Our Three Bears

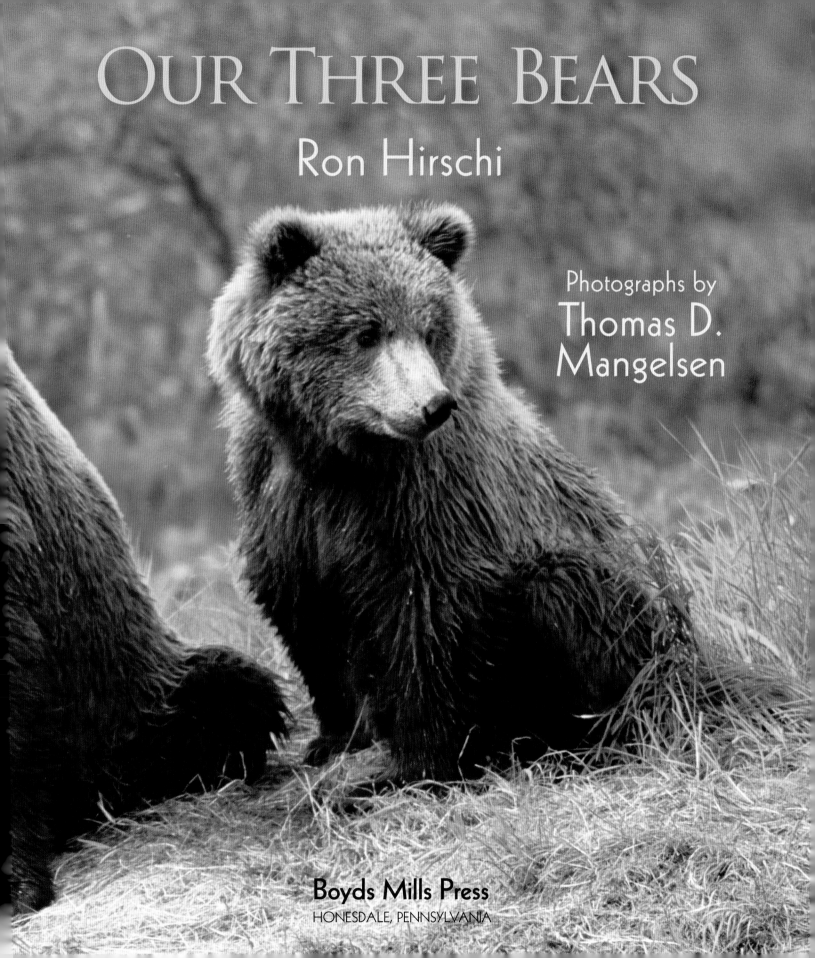

OUR THREE BEARS

Ron Hirschi

Photographs by
Thomas D.
Mangelsen

Boyds Mills Press
HONESDALE, PENNSYLVANIA

For Colton
 —R.H.

To David "Alex" and Matt,
for all the bears and wild places we have shared
 —T.M.

Text copyright © 2008 by Ron Hirschi
Photographs copyright © 2008 by Thomas D. Mangelsen

Boyds Mills Press, Inc.
815 Church Street
Honesdale, Pennsylvania 18431
Printed in China

Library of Congress Cataloging-in-Publication Data

Hirschi, Ron.
  Our three bears / by Ron Hirschi ; photographs by
Thomas D. Mangelsen. — 1st ed.
     p. cm.
  ISBN 978-1-59078-015-2 (hardcover : alk. paper)
  1. Bears—North America. 2. Bears—North America—
Pictorial works.
  I. Mangelsen, Thomas D. II. Title.
  QL737.C27H55 2008
  599.78097—dc22
                                    2007049380

First edition
The text of this book is set in 14-point Adobe Caslon.

10 9 8 7 6 5 4 3 2

Contents

BLACK BEAR

North America is home to many animals, none more exciting to watch than our three bears: black bear, grizzly bear, and polar bear. Each has adapted to natural habitats that range from the icy waters of the Alaskan and Canadian Arctic to the woodlands of the American Southeast. Each also faces special challenges as we change our world and theirs. We begin this look at their lives with the smallest and most abundant of the three, the black bear.

The path of a mother black bear and her cubs often leads through dense tangles of trees, shrubs, and swamps, making them difficult to observe. They might hunt by day, but many black bears are largely nocturnal, sniffing for food when the night sky is as dark as their glistening fur.

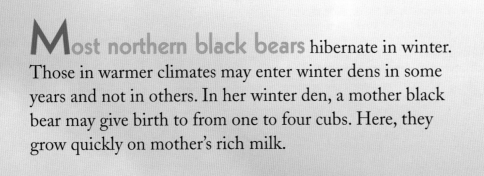

Most northern black bears hibernate in winter. Those in warmer climates may enter winter dens in some years and not in others. In her winter den, a mother black bear may give birth to from one to four cubs. Here, they grow quickly on mother's rich milk.

The Bear Facts

Black bears are the most widespread and by far the most abundant of our three bears. Their numbers are stable or even increasing in much of Canada, Alaska, and the western United States. They can also be found in Louisiana and Florida, as well as a good part of our eastern woodlands. Black bear numbers are far greater in the West, but populations are stable or increasing in Pennsylvania, New Jersey, and New York, where they might be seen just a short distance from heavily populated areas. How many black bears are there? Populations in the United States, Canada, and Mexico are difficult to estimate for many reasons, but scientists believe there may be as many as eight hundred thousand black bears in all of North America.

Black bears have fairly poor eyesight, but they have an excellent sense of smell. Their noses may lead them to natural food sources, including skunk cabbage, flowers, berries, fish, ants, squirrels, armadillos, and other small animals, as well as carrion. Their noses can also get them into trouble as they search campgrounds and cabins for food carelessly left behind by people.

When danger threatens, black bears young and old can climb a tree with ease. Once up a tree, they often stay in the high branches for several hours, waiting for the threat to pass.

The Bear Facts

Tiny at birth, black bear cubs weigh anywhere from 8 to 12 ounces, no more than a can of soda. Adult black bears can weigh more than 600 pounds but often range between 200 and 300 pounds.

Most black bears now live where they are the largest land predator. They can stroll through forests and fields, fearing no creature except human hunters. But even the biggest black bear cannot match the potential danger that comes from the much larger grizzly bear.

The Bear Facts

Excellent climbers, black bears can also run thirty miles per hour in short bursts, at least ten miles per hour faster than the fastest human. Black bears are also strong swimmers, often crossing ocean inlets through swift currents to reach islands in the Pacific Northwest.

GRIZZLY BEAR

Like great white sharks in the sea, grizzly bears roam western mountains as the most powerful predator, fearing no creature in its midst. Weighing as much as 1,700 pounds and standing as tall as ten feet, the grizzly may chase black bears from their food and from their cubs. Grizzlies attack and kill black bears, just as they sometimes kill other grizzlies.

If you follow a mother Alaskan brown bear (another name for grizzly bear), chances are good you will see her coax her cubs to learn how to fish for salmon. The fish swim in from the ocean to spawn in rivers, laying eggs in a nest of loose stones on the river bottom. The bears stand on the bank or leap in the water to snatch fish in their jaws or swat them from the rapids with paws bigger than a catcher's mitt.

13

These bright-colored salmon leap past falls and splash through riffles as they crowd into rivers. Bears usually live a solitary life. But the salmon feast is so inviting that the bears will gather close together to feed. Eagles, black bears, wolves, coyotes, and more than thirty other birds and mammals are also known to eat the flesh and eggs of spawning salmon. Even deer, which are prey to the grizzly, will slink to the riverbank to dine on the fish during spawning season.

Fat from the fish and their abundant, bright red eggs help the bears put on weight needed for their long winter ahead. The fish feast also helps cubs gain strength as they face survival challenges from adult male grizzlies. Fewer than five of every ten grizzly cubs live into adulthood.

South of Alaska, grizzly cubs born high in the Rocky Mountains of Montana, Wyoming,

and British Columbia learn to catch fish, too. Spawning trout are important food for these bears just as salmon are for Alaskan bears. But mother grizzly also leads her cubs through aspen woodlands and mountain meadows where elk calves are an important springtime prey.

Wolves (below) hunt these same mountains in packs, each wolf teaming with others to catch elk, deer, and moose. Not so the grizzly. The bear hunts alone, stalking its prey, then chasing it in a burst of speed as fast as that of a Kentucky Derby racehorse.

The Bear Facts

Hibernating bears don't eat, drink, urinate, defecate, or exercise during their winter sleep. A bear's normal heart rate of about one hundred beats per minute might drop to under ten. Other hibernators, including chipmunks, fall into a deeper sleep, and body temperatures drop to lower levels. No matter how an animal's body reacts to hibernation, this form of winter sleep helps them adapt when food is scarce and weather conditions are severe. A long siesta inside a snug den is often the best survival strategy.

Grizzly bears can also be sleepy bears. They might nap for an entire summer afternoon. When winter comes, bears sleep far longer as they hibernate in a slumber that might stretch from November to April. Since some grizzlies live to be thirty years or older, this means that a bear might sleep for a total of ten years during its lifetime.

The grizzly's strong front legs and long claws are important tools for catching prey, such as ground squirrels (below).

They also help the bear dig a winter den, often in root tangles at the base of a tree. The den is lined with branches and a blanket of soft moss.

During normal mountain winters, the den is covered by several feet of snow. Male bears den alone. Like black bears, grizzly mothers give birth to cubs in their winter dens. Two cubs are most common but as many as five might appear with their mother in spring.

The Bear Facts

Sometimes it's difficult to tell the difference between black bears and grizzly bears. Black bears are not always black. They can be brown, cinnamon, and even white. The grizzly's thick fur is usually golden brown and tipped, or grizzled, with a pale color. But they can also be black and often appear darker at a distance, which is where you want to be when observing them in the wild. The grizzly's shoulder hump and large, rounded face help distinguish it from the usually smaller black bear.

Weighing no more than a pound at birth, grizzly cubs grow quickly once spring arrives. They learn hunting and other survival skills from their mother and will den with her for about two years. At about three years of age, the cubs become more independent. Although it may not seem old in human terms, grizzlies usually become parents when they reach five or six years of age.

The Bear Facts

Grizzly bears roam mountainous regions of Montana, Wyoming, and Idaho. They are far more abundant in Russia, western Canada, and Alaska, where they are known as brown bears. The estimated grizzly/brown bear population is about 200,000, with more than 100,000 in Russia, about 25,000 in Canada, and about 33,000 in the United States, most of which are in Alaska. Though it has disappeared from California, the grizzly bear remains on the state's flag. It's still California's animal mascot, too, even though there are as many as 20,000 black bears in the state.

The Bear Facts

Individual female grizzly bears live in an area of about 300 square miles, while males cover much greater distances, requiring as many as 1,500 square miles in their lifetime. The bears need wilderness habitat to roam safely for their survival and for humans to feel safe, too—for themselves and their cattle, sheep, and other domestic animals.

In places such as Yellowstone
National Park, grizzly populations are expanding.
It remains to be seen if young, independent
grizzlies will find safe homes outside the park
boundaries. No matter what path they take, their
journey is much more difficult now as highways,
homes, and ranches reach higher into the
mountains of the West.

The Bear Facts

The grizzly's diet is a surprising mix of plant and animal food. The same bears that chase elk in the spring often dine for days on end on tiny moths or the seeds of whitebark pines in autumn. They also dig ground squirrels from burrows and catch trout as they gather to spawn in streams. In addition to elk and deer, the grizzly also preys on moose and bison.

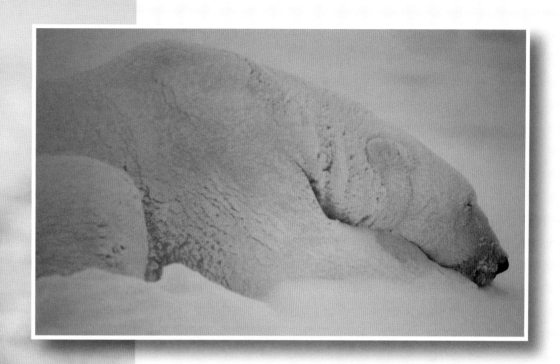

POLAR BEAR

Far to the north, polar bears roam their Arctic world, which is home to so few people that they rarely, if ever, encounter a human. The bears hunt for seals, their favorite meal. They stalk their prey on solid sheets of sea ice. The great white bears also silently wait and stare for hours, even days, at holes in the ice, then snatch seals when they pop up to take a breath of air.

Mother polar bears spend a great deal
of time with their cubs. Unlike other bears, only
female polar bears hibernate. Bears that are about
to give birth dig a safe winter den where an average
of two little ones are born. The cubs nurse through
the long Arctic nights and dark days, growing on
mother's rich milk until they emerge in the spring.

Follow the path of a female polar bear with cub
and your long journey will cross ice, open sea, and tundra
as far from city lights as any place on earth. The search
for food may take the bears several miles from the ocean,
but the animals are highly adapted to life at the sea edge.

As a grizzly bear would travel by land for many miles,
polar bears readily cross open bodies of water. Tremendous
swimmers, adult polar bears will dive into the water and come
out onto ice or land more than fifty miles away. Tiring from a
swim of much less distance, a cub will cry out to its mother,
who often helps the little ones with a ride on her back.

Like black bears and grizzly bears, polar bear cubs are tiny at birth but grow quickly.

Highly protective, polar bear mothers scold, cuddle, and teach their young after the family leaves the birthing den. The cubs gradually learn to hunt and feed on seals. But a mother polar bear eats most of what she kills, especially in the cubs' first year. Fat from seal blubber is turned into milk in her body as the cubs continue to nurse, sometimes into their second year, when they might weigh 200 pounds or more.

The Bear Facts

Scientists classify polar bears as marine mammals. Their scientific name, *Ursus maritimus*, or sea bear, reflects their aquatic way of life. They have keen underwater eyesight. Their long, powerful front legs and large paddlelike paws help them swim with ease. When diving into water, the polar bear's nostrils close tight and its ears lie back, adding to the bear's streamlined shape and swimming abilities.

olar bears are most closely related

to the grizzly, from which they are believed to have evolved some two hundred thousand years ago when ice sheets covered much more of the earth's northern reaches. In this harsh environment, natural selection favored many creatures with white coats. The polar bear's coloration is one reflection of its adaptation to this icy landscape, but the polar bear evolved in many other ways. Like the grizzly, polar bears maintained a keen sense of smell and great strength. But the polar bear is unlike its relative in one significant way—its close ties to the sea.

The Bear Facts

The polar bear's fur is transparent, reflecting light to make the animal appear creamy or white, much like the color of snow. A dense insulating layer of fur is covered by much longer guard hairs. These hairs are hollow and act like thousands of tiny flotation devices. They make the bears more buoyant in the water and help them to shake dry after a swim.

The polar bear's Arctic world is a vast, mostly treeless place completely covered by ice and snow in winter months. This changes dramatically when temperatures rise and ice turns to open sea. Spring is the critical season for hungry bears. If sea ice lasts into spring, it means solid footing for bears to stalk seals, one of their most important food sources.

Polar bears usually hunt alone, feeding on seals as well as walrus, kelp, berries, bird eggs, and carcasses of beached whales. Ravens with glistening black feathers dip and roll as they dive from the air to snatch scraps from a polar bear meal. Arctic foxes (above) will also follow polar bears, sometimes for weeks at a time. The much smaller fox keeps a safe distance from the bear's sharp claws and then darts in to sneak a meal.

Polar bears will fight over food
and are solitary much of their lives. But they also
gather together peacefully at times, especially
when they have plenty to eat. Large gatherings
are especially common when whales beach
themselves, providing a large food supply that
can feed many bears for days or weeks.

At other times, polar bears play-fight and
even stomp their hind legs and spread their
forelegs to dance a kind of polar bear dance.
A dance and hug may lead to partnerships, mainly
between young males who will travel, hunt,
and sleep together for several months. Females,
especially those with cubs, typically avoid contact
with other bears. They remain with courting males
for only a brief time, as few as one to three days.

The Bear Facts

The largest land predators on earth,
polar bears can stand more than eleven
feet high and weigh more than 1,700
pounds. They typically reside in and
return to familiar areas, but they are also
great wanderers. It is estimated that a
single polar bear may cover an area of
about one hundred thousand square
miles in its lifetime. This is an immense
amount of space. Imagine an area
of land that is twenty-five miles wide
and stretches all the way from Seattle,
Washington, to Miami, Florida. The
estimated polar bear population ranges
from twenty thousand to twenty-five
thousand. Twelve thousand to fifteen
thousand of these live in Canada.

While their enormous size and strength bring fear to animals and humans who encounter them in the wild, polar bears can show wondrous curiosity toward other creatures. They have been observed nose to nose with sled dogs, as if they wish to know more about this animal that has long been a companion to humans. Maybe it is time to protect our three bears in the same way we protect our dogs and other pets from harm.

The Bear Facts

Fat reserves help the polar bear stay warm. The Arctic sun sets in mid-October and does not rise again until the middle of February. During this period, temperatures never climb above and often stay below freezing. The bear's fat layer also helps it go without food for as long as eight months. These same fat reserves make it difficult to stay cool if temperatures in July rise above freezing. Sometimes temperatures can reach 50 degrees Fahrenheit or higher, which is quite warm for the Arctic.

FINAL TRACKS

I remember well the excitement of seeing my first bear with my grandfather many years ago. We were picking huckleberries in a forest clearing on the Olympic Peninsula, not far from where I live today. I am happy to report that black bears still live in that same area and the surrounding trees in that forest have grown a good one hundred feet in height in the forty or so years since we watched the bear together.

Over the years, I've had the chance to spend many hours watching black bears and grizzlies, sometimes in unusual locations. I now live on a small island, and black bears often swim across swift ocean channels to reach our shores. At first sight, they look like black Labrador retrievers as they swim and shake off on the beach.

I've also had the good fortune to work with Tom Mangelsen, one of the most observant, concerned, and skilled bear photographers in the world. Tom has spent many years photographing black, grizzly, and polar bears and has a special love for these creatures that hold such wonder for people of all ages.

Tom and I both hope you enjoy this book. Even more important, we hope you take the time to get to know more about the bears and their world by visiting places that support bears in a way that sustains their populations into the future. You can see black bears in many western national parks, including Olympic, Yosemite, Glacier, Yellowstone, and Mount Rainier in the United States and Jasper and Banff in Canada. While populations are not as great in the Midwest and eastern United States, your chances of seeing a black bear are good in Great Smoky Mountains National Park near the Tennessee–North Carolina border and in Voyageurs National Park in Minnesota.

Grizzly bears are not as easy to find, mainly because of their rarity. Most good Internet research sites display maps of where grizzlies once lived and where they live today. That comparison shows how little room they have left to roam. But many people work hard to ensure that existing populations remain and thrive in places such as Yellowstone and Glacier national parks in the United States and in much of Alaska and western British Columbia. You will surely see both black and brown bears if you head to a salmon stream in Alaska during spawning season.

Polar bears live in a land not easily reached by most people, but guided trips are available to polar bear viewing locations in northern Manitoba and the Northwest Territories in Canada. Most scientists fear the polar bear's future as global warming helps to melt more Arctic ice each year. This reduces solid ice that the polar bears need for their hunting surface—for their very survival.

Manitoba has led efforts to protect polar bears in Canada by creating the Polar Bear Protection Act of 2002. The province also encourages the development of clean-energy facilities. Scientists warn that these alternatives to fossil fuels are needed to stop global warming and protect polar bear habitat as well as our own.

Whatever path you follow on your outdoor adventures, chances of seeing a black bear are far greater than seeing a grizzly. Grizzly sightings are not the most common, and your chance of seeing a polar bear in the wild is not great at all. Even if you never see any of our three bears, chances are good that you will care deeply for their future. Humans have long held bears of all kinds in the highest regard. We hope this respect will help scientists find a path we can follow that enables us to protect the needs of black, grizzly, and polar bears into our uncertain future.

It is good to know that black bears are increasing in numbers in many parts of the United States. Recent efforts by scientists have also helped grizzly bear numbers increase, especially in and near Yellowstone National Park. Polar bears are in far more serious trouble, and they will likely become the first living creature to be placed on the endangered species list as a result of global warming. Because this threat comes directly from humans, the polar bear's future is in our hands, yours and mine.

Index

For More Information

The following organizations in Canada and the United States are working hard to protect our three bears. Check their Web sites* to learn about their activities.

Canadian Parks and Wilderness Society: www.cpaws.org
Center for Biological Diversity: www.biologicaldiversity.org
Greater Yellowstone Coalition: www.greateryellowstone.org
Grizzly Bear Alliance: www.grizzlybearalliance.org
North American Bear Center: www.bear.org
Polar Bears International: www.polarbearsinternational.org
Vital Ground: www.vitalground.org
Wildsight: www.wildsight.ca

*Web sites active at time of publication

Further Reading

For Young Readers
Hirschi, Ron. *Searching for Grizzlies*. Photographs by Thomas D. Mangelsen. Honesdale, PA: Boyds Mills Press, 2005.
Leeson, Tom, and Pat Leeson. *Black Bear*. Woodbridge, CT: Blackbirch Press, 2000.
Miller, Debbie S. *A Polar Bear Journey*. Photographs by Jon Van Zyle. Boston: Little, Brown, 1997.
Stonehouse, Bernard. *Bears: A Visual Introduction to Bears*. Photographs by Martin Camm. New York: Checkmark, 1998.

For Older Readers
Mangelsen, Thomas D. *Polar Dance: Born of the North Wind*. Story by Fred Bruemmer. Omaha, NE: Images of Nature, 1997.
Schullery, Paul. *The Bears of Yellowstone*. Worland, WY: High Plains Publishing, 1992.